Exploring Materials

Plastic

Abby Colich

Raintree is an imprint of Capstone Global Library Limited, a company incorporated in England and Wales having its registered office at 7 Pilgrim Street, London, EC4V 6LB Registered company number: 6695582

To contact Raintree:
Phone: 0845 6044371
Fax: + 44 (0) 1865 312263
Email: myorders@raintreepublishers.co.uk
Outside the UK please telephone +44 1865 312262

Text © Capstone Global Library Limited 2014
First published in hardback in 2014
The moral rights of the proprietor have been asserted.

Edited by Abby Colich, Daniel Nunn, and Catherine Veitch
Designed by Marcus Bell
Picture research by Tracy Cummins
Production by Victoria Fitzgerald
Originated by Capstone Global Library Ltd
Printed and bound in China by Leo Paper Products Ltd

ISBN 978 1 4062 6334 3
17 16 15 14 13
10 9 8 7 6 5 4 3 2 1

British Library Cataloguing in Publication Data
Colich, Abby.
Plastic. – (Exploring materials)
620.1'923-dc23
A full catalogue record for this book is available from the British Library.

Acknowledgements
We would like to thank the following for permission to reproduce photographs: Alamy p. 11 (© Ronald Karpilo); Corbis (© David McLain/Aurora Photo); Getty Images pp. 4 (© commerceandculturestock), 7, 14 (© KidStock), 9, 23b (© Win McNamee), 10 (© Jupiterimages), 18 (© altrendo images), 19 (© Geri Lavrov), 23c (© Jupiterimages); Shutterstock pp. 5 (© Alinute Silzeviciute), 6a (© Gualberto Becerra), 6b (© Alexander Dashewsky), 6c (© Michaelstockfoto), 6d (© krugloff), 12 (© Dmitriy Shironosov), 13 (© Jari Hindström), 15 (© VIPDesignUSA), 17 (© Stocksnapper), 20 (© Chamille White), 21 (© Photogrape), 22 (© Africa Studio, © Denis Vrublevsk, © Kostenko Maxim) 23a (© Stocksnapper); Superstock p. 16 (© Tetra Images).

Front cover photograph of a girl playing with interlocking blocks reproduced with permission of Superstock (© Fancy Collection).

Back cover photograph reproduced with permission of Shutterstock (© VIPDesignUSA).

We would like to thank Valarie Akerson, Nancy Harris, Dee Reid, and Diana Bentley for their assistance in the preparation of this book.

Every effort has been made to contact copyright holders of material reproduced in this book. Any omissions will be rectified in subsequent printings if notice is given to the publisher.

Contents

What is plastic?

Plastic is a material.

Materials are what things are made from.

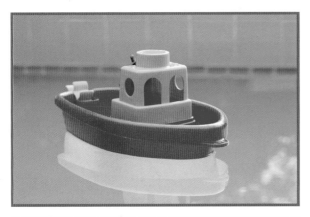

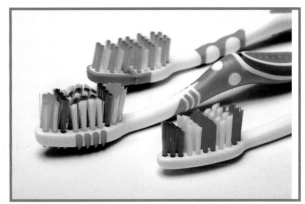

Plastic has many uses.

We use plastic to make many
different things.

Where does plastic come from?

Plastic is made by people.

oil

Plastic is made from oil.

Plastic can be recycled or reused.

Recycled plastic can be used to make new things.

What is plastic like?

Plastic can be coloured or clear.

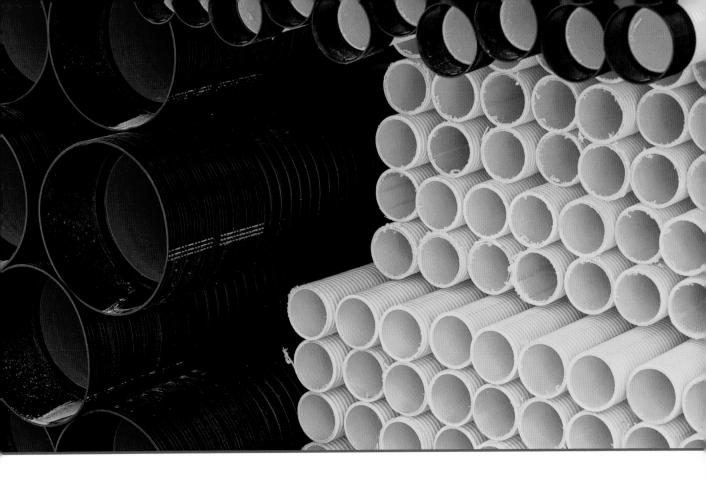

Plastic can be thick or thin.

smooth →

Plastic can be smooth or bumpy.

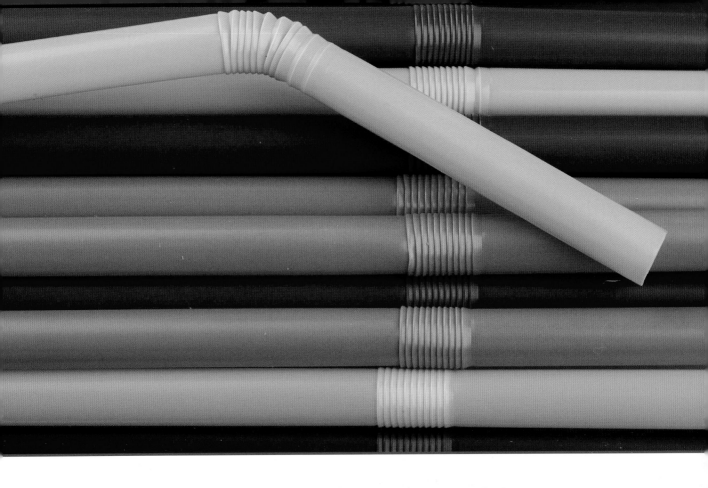

Plastic can bend and change shape.

How do we use plastic?

We use plastic when we eat
and drink.

container →

We use plastic containers to store things.

Some toys are made from plastic.

Some bags are made from plastic.

bicycle helmet

sunglasses

Plastic can keep us safe.

Plastic is used in many places.

Quiz

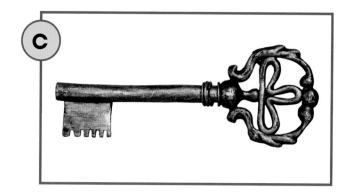

Which of these things are made of plastic?

Answer on page 24.

Picture glossary

 **container** something used to store things

 **oil** slippery liquid that does not mix with water

 **recycle** make used items into new things

Index

> The **letters (a)** and **beach toys (b)** are made of plastic.

Notes for parents and teachers

Before reading

Ask children if they have heard the term "material" and what they think it means. Reinforce the concept of materials. Explain that all objects are made from different materials. A material is something that takes up space and can be used to make other things. Ask children to give examples of different materials. These may include glass, plastic, and rubber.

To get children interested in the topic, ask if they know what plastic is. Identify any misconceptions they may have. Ask them to think about whether their ideas might change as the book is read.

After reading

- Check to see if any of the identified misconceptions have changed.
- Show the children examples of plastic, including plastic toys, bags, and bottles.
- Pass the plastic objects round the children. Ask them to describe the properties of each object. What colour is it? Is it hard? Does it bend? Is it heavy or light? Ask them to name other items made from plastic.